LEARNING

IN OUTER

SPACE

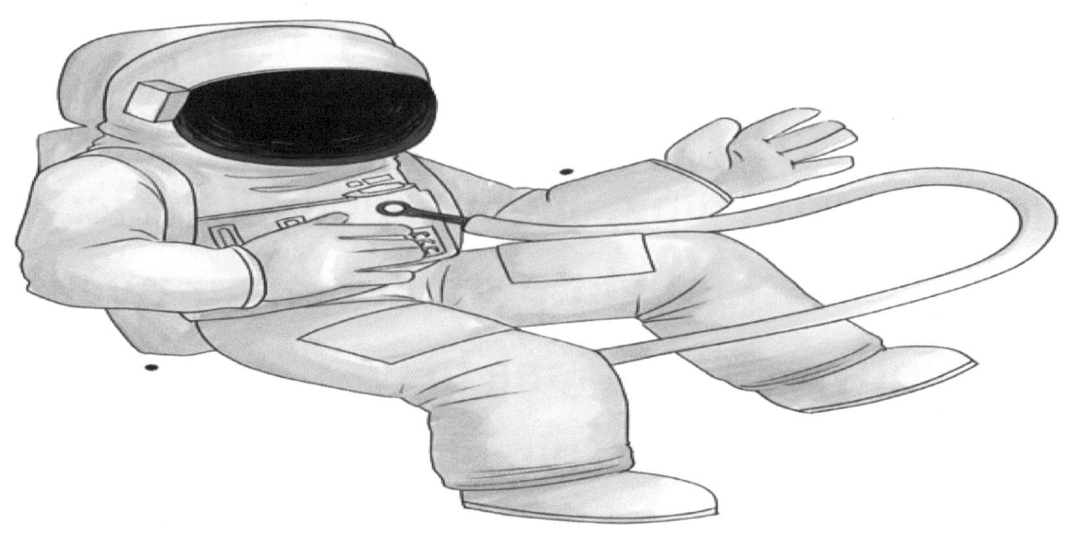

ABOUT THE AUTHOR:

My name is Charlene Hendrix Brady. I am a former preschool educator, mother of one son, and a grandmother of two little ones. I enjoyed seeing children learn by reading, singing, and all basic learning activities. I taught preschool over twenty years. Presently, I'm engaging in writing young children's educational learning books. My hobbies are reading, writing, going to church, volunteering in the community, watching sports, and playing with my grandchildren.

Today we will pretend to go to outer space.

Do you want to go with the astronauts to outer space?

Okay, great!

Put on your space suit.

Now put on your air tank and helmet.....

because there is no
air in space.

Is everybody ready?

Let's go!

Everyone get inside of the space shuttle!

Please sit down and put on your seat belts.

Let's count down....

10... 9... 8... 7... 6...

5... 4... 3... 2... 1...

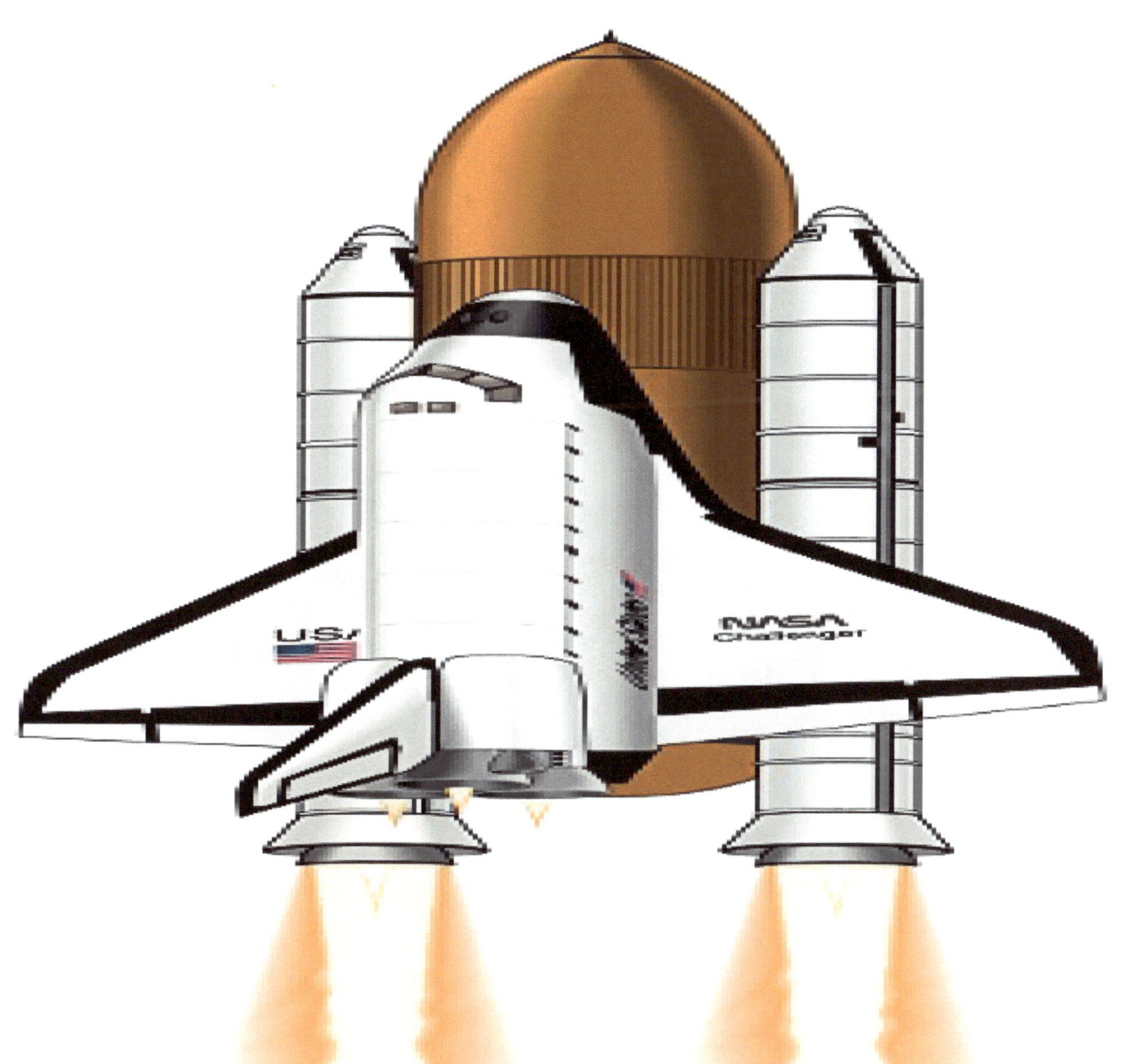

Blast off!!!!

Off we go to outer space!

We can see stars.

Yayyyy! We made it!

Now follow along to see what is here.

The astronauts see a green alien in outer space.

Let's take a picture with the alien.

The alien is nice.

The astronaut took a picture with the alien.

This is the alien family.

We took a picture with
them.

There is no gravity on the moon.

The astronaut floats while in the space.

Can you float like the astronaut?

Good job little astronauts!

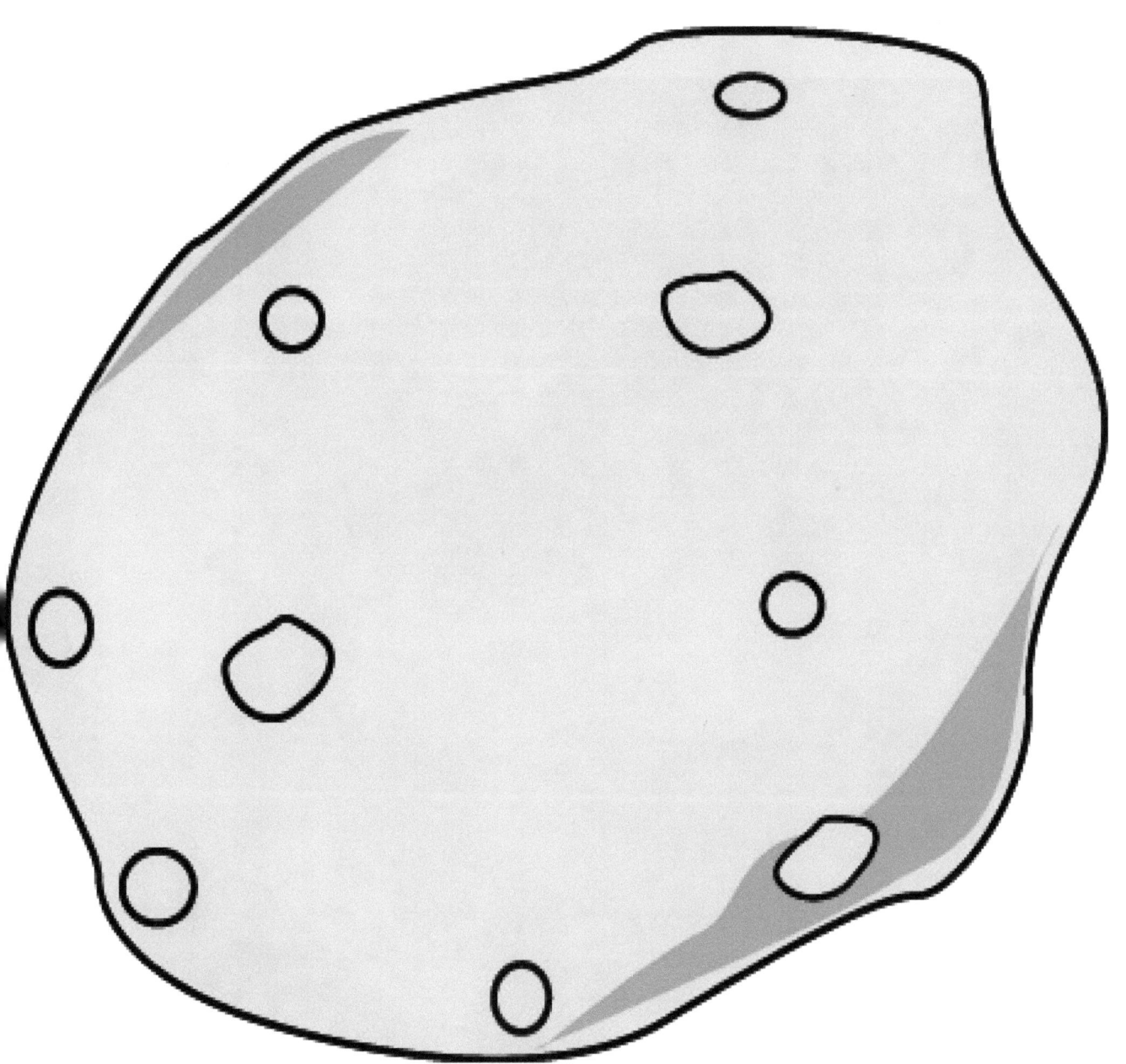

There are asteroids in outer space.

We can see the earth from outer space.

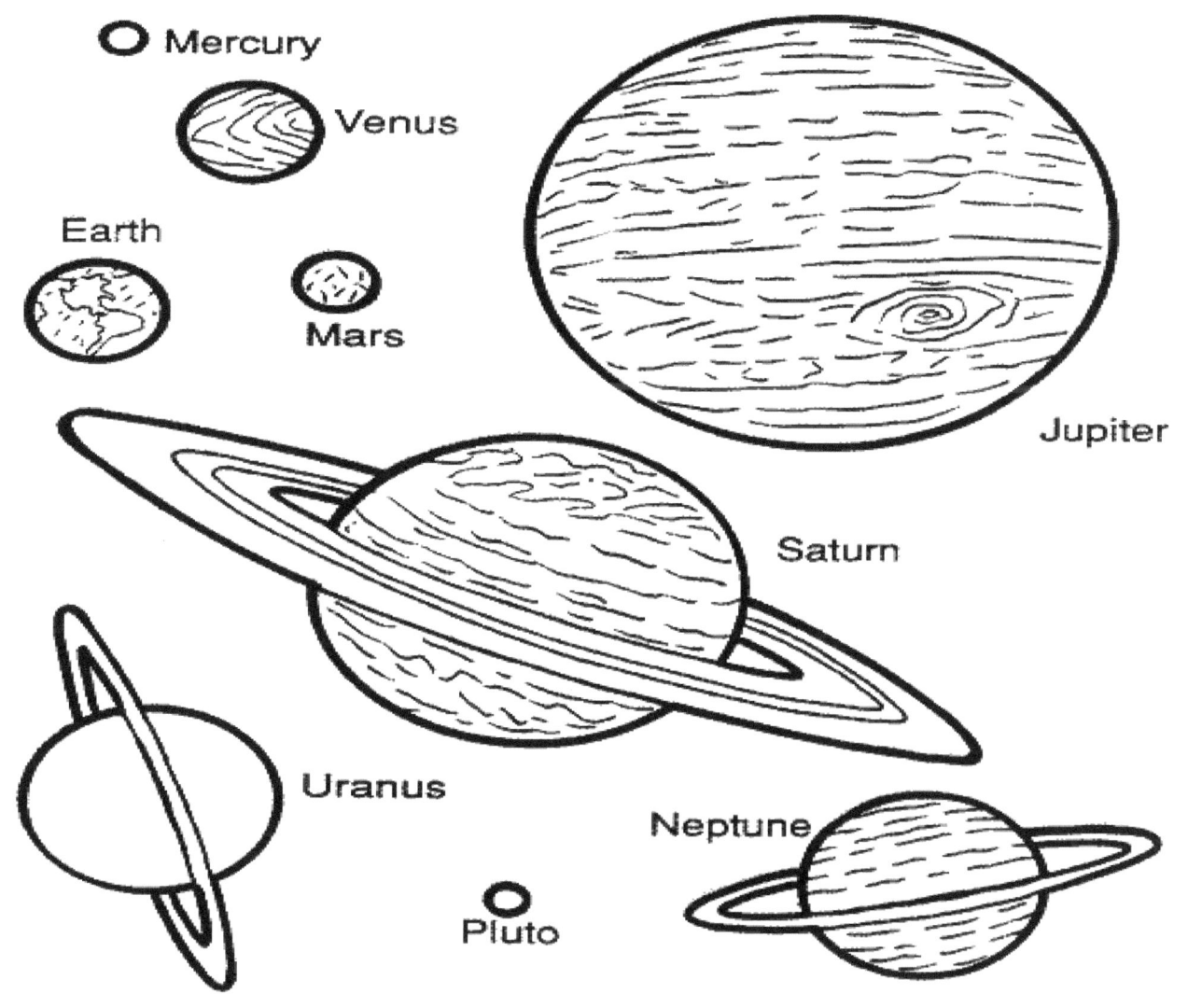

Mercury

Venus

Earth

Mars

Jupiter

Saturn

Uranus

Neptune

Pluto

We can see other planets from outer space.

It's cold here in outer space.

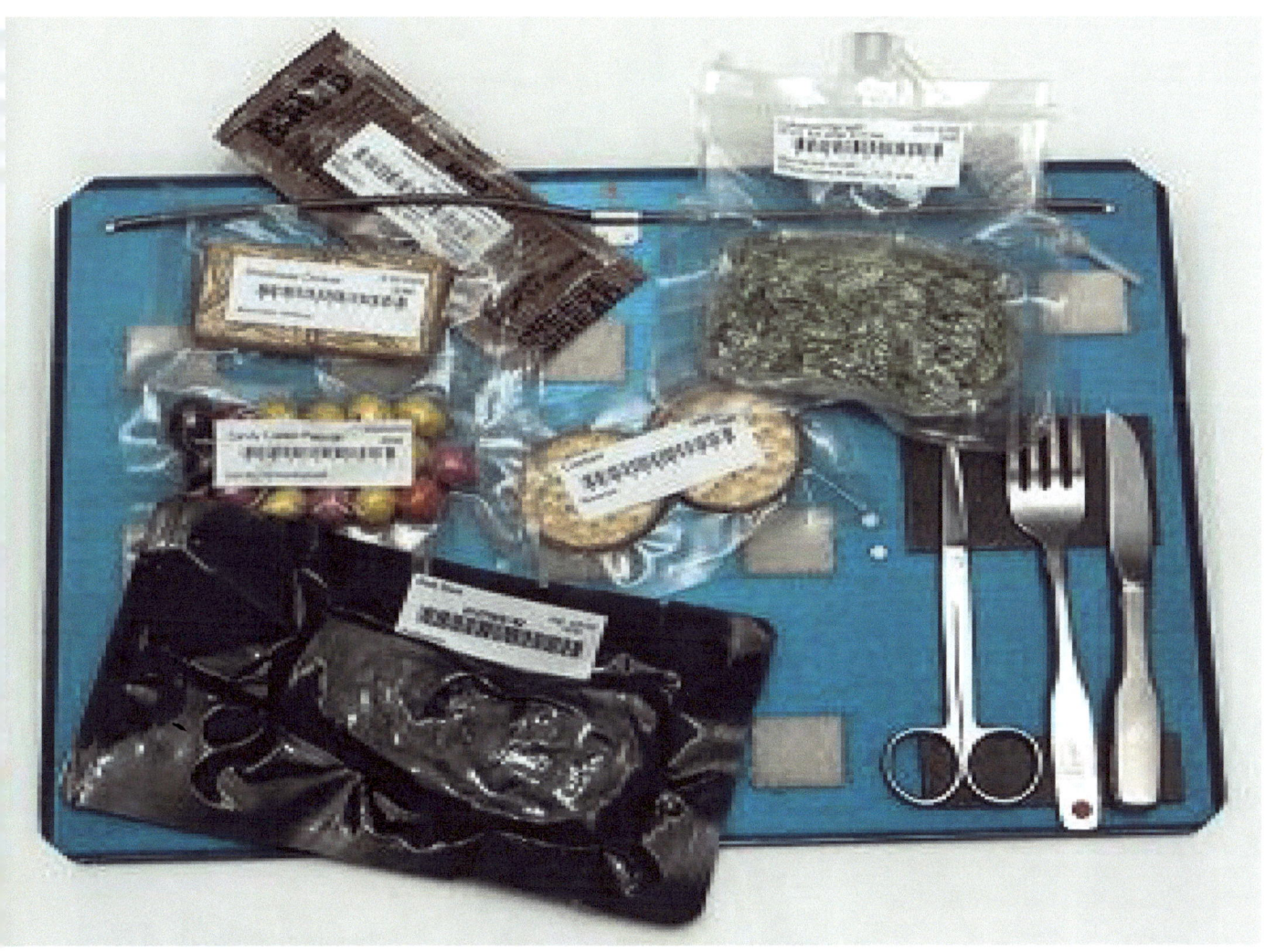

There are no restaurants in space. We bring our food with us from Earth.

There are no stores or school in outer space.

Two aliens riding in a flying saucer

The astronauts can see the moon from outer space.

The astronaut leaves a flag on outer space.

We had a blast in outer space!

Time to go home!

A spooky alien waves
bye to the astronauts.

The astronauts are back inside the space ship.

Yayyyyyy!

We made it back safe.

Did you have fun with the astronauts while in outer space?

Great!!!!

..... Thank you for coming along and for being an awesome little astronaut!

The End